The Black Eyed Child of Cannock Chase

by

Lee Brickley

Introduction

Up until late September in 2014, very few people knew my name. A self-published author with only one book under my belt, I had done little to warrant the international media attention I was about to receive. For you see, my first book, entitled *UFOs Werewolves & The Pig-Man,* had been published a year earlier. It contained details of a terrifying paranormal encounter that took place on Cannock Chase in Staffordshire during the early 1980s. One of my own family members had claimed to see an unsightly and downright spooky black-eyed child.

For reasons I'll never quite understand, a good friend and reporter from the Birmingham Mail newspaper decided to pick up on the story. He also found a couple of more recent reports on my blog and used them for an article he was writing. After checking my emails many weeks later, I found that he had tried to contact me for information before the story went to print. I didn't notice that at the time, so it was a nice surprise to see my face in the newspapers on Monday 29th September 2014.

What happened next was completely unexpected.

From his short and accurate 1000 word story came literally thousands of others.

I could type the words "black-eyed child" into Google search, filter by date and see hundreds more every time I refreshed the page. Needless to say, I was completely overwhelmed by the attention this case received from the press, but I decided to go with it. In one week I had spoken live on no less than 8 different BBC radio stations, and the story made the front-page of the Daily Star tabloid newspaper no less than five times.

The online world lit up with people posting their theories and commenting on the news that black-eyed children reports were on the rise around the world. Indeed, I believe one front-page headline used the word "plague". All that from a little article in the Birmingham Mail.

Even though the press has stopped talking about it now, I still get sighting reports of the black eyed child almost every month.

In this book, I've included some of the most interesting and terrifying sighting reports from 2013 right through to 2020. Prepare to be frightened, and remember, don't go out after dark!

Birches Valley

Date: **10th July 2013**

Time: **1:30pm**

Location: **Birches Valley, Hednesford**

Sighting report:

Around 2 months ago my daughter and I were walking through Birches Valley when we heard the screams of a young child. I couldn't tell if it was a boy or a girl, but they definitely seemed in distress and sounded very close to us, so we instantly started running towards the noise.

We couldn't find the child anywhere and so stopped to catch our breath, that's when I turned round and saw a girl standing behind me, no more than 10 years old, with her hands over her eyes, like she was waiting for a birthday cake.

I asked if she was okay and if she had been the one screaming, she then put her arms down by her side and opened her eyes, which is when I saw they were completely black, no iris, no white, nothing.

I jumped back and grabbed my daughter, when I looked again, the child was gone. It was strange really, I knew something was going to happen, even before it did, I just had a weird feeling.

Stile Cop

Date: **13th September 2014**

Time: **04:10am**

Location: **Stile Cop, Hednesford**

Sighting report:

On Saturday 13th September, my wife and I were walking though Cannock Chase near Stile Cop with our dog.

Once we had entered the woodland, and the road was no longer visible, we started to hear the giggling noise of a little girl.

To our amazement, a child, no taller than one meter in height appeared as if out of nowhere further up the path in front of us. We stopped dead in our tracks after noticing her eyes had no colour. Her head was tilted to the side in much the same way it would appear if she had been hung.

She stared at us for around five minutes before running away into a densely grouped area of trees. My wife wanted to follow her, but I was having none of it. She thinks I'm silly telling everyone about this now, even though she was terrified at the time.

Heath Hayes Village

Date: **10th May 2015**

Time: **11:54pm**

Location: **Heath Hayes Village**

Sighting report:

I was walking home from my job at a local care home on the evening of 10th May when I saw the strangest thing. I walked down Heath Hayes high street towards the Spar shop (I know that is a different shop now), when I heard a strange scratching noise coming from between two of the buildings on my left-hand side. It's a row of shops with some flats above, and there is a small access alleyway the residents use to get inside. Anyway, this scratching noise…

I couldn't really see much to begin with because it was really dark out, and the alleyway isn't very wide. The noise caught my attention and so I went in for a closer look.

I presumed I would see a fox or something similar because there are loads of them around Heath Hayes these days. I wish I had seen a fox to be fair because what I'm about to tell you is going to make me seem crazy.

So, as I walked towards the noise, I began to see a silhouette in the alleyway. It wasn't very large and so I presumed it was a child or a small woman. I kicked something on the floor - maybe a can or something similar, and it made a noise. In an instant, the silhouette spun around and I saw the blackest eyes I've ever seen. These weren't just black, they were jet black. They were "emptiness of the universe" black, and it terrified me.

Scared, I immediately turned around and moved away from the alleyway. I tried to gather my thoughts and quickly realised what I was looking at in the alleyway was a child. That's why the silhouette had seemed so small. She must have been wearing some kind of dark dress because I could hardly see it. All I saw was black hair, and the blackest eyes ever.

I can't explain this properly with words, but those eyes pulled me in. It was like she was looking deep into my soul, and she knew everything about me. My deepest and most secret fears. Honestly, this was one of the most horrendous experiences of my life. I still felt all shook up more than a week later. When I got a safe distance away from the alleyway, I turned around to see if the black eyed girl followed me, but she didn't.

Every time I walk past that alley I take a look inside to see if there is anything there. Thankfully there hasn't been anything since.

Rumer Hill Estate

Date: **20th October 2015**

Time: **01:15am**

Location: **Rumer Hill Estate, Cannock**

Sighting report:

I'd been around to see some mates in a flat on Rumer Hill. We'd all had a bit of a smoke and spent the night playing on the PS3. At about 1am, I decided it was time to get off home, and so I grabbed my things, said goodbye, and walked out of the door. My friend's flat is on Devon Green, and so I only had to walk about 200 metres before I'd be off the estate entirely. The thing is; I didn't make it that far.

As I walked down the road towards the chip-shop on Rumer Hill, I saw this little girl run across the road in front of me and down behind the flats. There's a little road that doesn't go anywhere. It just leads to behind the flats where there are some garages, but it's a dead end. Anyway, she moved so fast that it all felt really odd, and so I decided I'd walk around there and see where she was going.

I thought it probably wasn't safe for her to be outside at that time either.

I walked down the little side road that goes behind the flats, and as I did, all the street lights that would usually illuminate the area went out. It was freaky. It really was. I turned the corner to where the garages are and everything was pitch black. I couldn't see my hand in front of my face, but just then, I heard a little girl giggle. It sent shivers up my spine for some reason, but I told myself it was the little girl I'd seen run across the road so I thought being scared was irrational.

I called out to her and asked if she knew how to get back to her mummy and daddy or if she needed help being as the street lights had gone out, but everything just went silent. No more giggling, no reply, no nothing. I asked again, but heard no reply.

Presuming the girl was shy and didn't want to talk to me, I decided I would continue my walk home but call the police on the way and let them know what I'd seen, and that there might be a child there who needed taking home.

As I turned around, I had the shock of my life as the little giggling girl whom I'd followed was now standing right in front of me. No more than two metres. She was looking towards the ground, and wearing some kind of dirty white dress that looked a hundred years old. She had black greasy or wet hair and she remained perfectly still.

I immediately told her she startled me and asked again if she wanted any help. I could only see her because of the light of the moon - she was in just the right position to stand out against the darkness.

Another moment of silence passed before the girl began to slowly lift her head, and it was then I saw something really weird about her face. She had black eyes. Not a little bit black you understand, but totally black. No whites, no iris, just black. It felt like she stared through me rather than at me and I was instantly frozen.

I'd have probably stayed there frozen forever were it not for what happened next. Still staring into my soul, the girl opened her mouth and let out a noise like I've never heard before. It was like a high-pitched scream. Like a dog-whistle-scream almost? I don't know how else to describe it, sorry.

As she did that, the street lights all came on at the same time really bright, and many of the bulbs seemed to blow as I saw sparks falling onto the street. That distracted my eyes for a fraction of a second, and when I looked back towards where the girl stood in front of me, there was nothing there. She was gone.

Needless to say, all my mates think I had too much to smoke or something like that, but I honestly didn't. This really happened.

Barnard Way

Date: **8th January 2016**

Time: **02:35am**

Location: **Barnard Way, Cannock**

Sighting report:

You know Barnard Way in Cannock? I always walk through there when my shift finishes at work, and every three weeks, I have to work lates. That means I don't get out of the factory until 2am and I have to do the walk of shame right through the centre of town. The only people I usually see are either drunk or going to score drugs. The only cars on the road are taxi drivers, drug dealers, and police. Everyone else has usually been in bed for ages, so it's quiet out there.

This one night, I was about half way home, walking through Barnard Way when I saw this girl just standing in the middle of the road in front of me. There were houses on my right-hand side, and a small field on my left. All the lights were off in the houses though as it was so late.

The girl shocked me because I'd been walking with my head down listening to music, so I didn't even notice her until I was about ten feet away.

I stopped instantly when I saw her because if I'd carried on walking I'd have bumped into her about three seconds later. I stopped to let her pass really. It was only then my eyes focused on her properly and I realised something wasn't right. This girl was about ten years old, and she looked ill to be honest. Her skin was really pale, her hair looked like she never washed it, and her clothes were filthy. I was about to call a homeless shelter or something until I noticed her eyes.

They were like holes in her face. Totally black like you wouldn't believe. It was like she didn't even have eyes there at all. Just this deep abyss that seemed to carry on forever and never let any light in. My heart began to beat fast.

I asked if she was okay, still stood frozen in position, and she didn't say a word. She didn't move at all. She just stood there for a moment and then lifted her left arm to shoulder height and pointed at me.

You really aren't going to believe this, but when she did that, I flew backwards. It was like someone massive had just punched me in the chest. My feet definitely left the ground as I fell over backwards and landed on my arse.

I felt like I'd just been in the ring with Mike Tyson when I finally got back to my feet. I don't know if I was knocked out for a little while or what, but I looked around for the black eyed child and she was gone.

There's something cool though. You know she pointed at me and I flew backwards? Well, there is a purple stain on the white shirt I was wearing that night in exactly the position where I felt the force strike. I've tried getting it out over and over again, and it won't budge. I don't drink wine, and there's no reason I'd have a purple stain there. Weird ay?

Cross Keys

Date: **23rd June 2016**

Time: **04:10am**

Location: **Cross Keys, Hednesford**

Sighting report:

I was walking home from Hednesford to Heath Hayes past the Cross Keys pub one evening a couple of weeks ago when I became scared to my very core. I wasn't paying much attention to the few cars that passed, and the walk was pretty quiet up until I got near the turning for Hednesford Football stadium. It looked like there was a little girl just standing in the middle of the road.

I shouted to ask if she needed any assistance, but she didn't reply. She was facing in the opposite direction you see. I started walking closer to her and called out again. The moment I did that, she turned around silently to face me. It was pretty dark outside but I could clearly see she was wearing some weird clothes. She looked like something out of the 1800s. A sort of white lace dress with something black on top of it. It's hard to describe.

Her eyes were closed when she turned around, but when she opened them I almost fell over. Her eyes were as black as the night and that's no lie. I'd never seen anything like it. I thought maybe she'd taken some drugs or something, and so I asked again if she needed any help.

The girl walked forwards, reached out, and put her hand on my chest. It felt freezing cold, like it was made of ice. It hurt my chest, even though she was only touching me through my shirt. I looked into her eyes again and saw that she wasn't on drugs. They just didn't look right, but I know kids buy those contact lens things these days, so I presumed it must be that.

The next thing I know, it's 7am, I'm lying on the grass at the side of the road by the island, the girl is nowhere to be seen, and there are about a hundred cars full of people driving past me on their way to work. I have absolutely no idea what happened.

Newlands Lane

Date: **31st October 2016**

Time: **01:00am**

Location: **Newlands Lane, Heath Hayes**

Sighting report:

I was walking my dog down Newlands Lane in Heath Hayes when I saw something I'm almost nervous to tell you about. The lane has been blocked at the bottom for years, and it's all overgrown, but my dog loves to explore that bit of the lane, and so I walked all the way down.

I had my torch obviously because it was so late, but the only other light came from the stars. As usual, my dog ran into the overgrown area of the lane, probably looking for rabbits or something. I waited for him to come back, but he was taking a while, and so I called his name.

As I did, I heard my dog let out a bit of a whimper like he was scared. So, I called his name again, and sure enough, he came running back towards me.

What was weird was that the dog then cowered behind me, and he never normally does that.

I heard a rustle in front of me from where the dog had just come, and so I lifted my torch up to see if I could work out what it was. I thought maybe there was a fox or something and that's why the dog got scared.

In front of me was a child. A little girl, about ten years old maybe. I want to say she looked like a regular child, but she really didn't. Even at first glance I could see her skin was incredibly white and her face looked emotionless.

I didn't say anything, and neither did she. I just stayed there perfectly still shining my torch in her direction for a few seconds. I didn't really know what to do. Suddenly my torch stopped working. Everything went black. I pressed the button over and over, but it wouldn't switch on.

The next thing I knew, I felt something brush against my hand. Thinking it was the dog, I bent down slightly. As I did that, my torch started working again and I jumped a mile as I saw it was the little girl holding out her hand near mine. I almost had a heart attack. I finally spoke and asked who she was.

The girl brushed her cold hand against mine again and moved in even closer. This was when I noticed her eyes were black. It was like she didn't even have eyeballs. They were just like two holes in her face. I shouted something sweary, the dog barked loudly, and the girl quickly disappeared.

The thing is, it's not like she ran away or something like that. She moved upwards. From the ground in front of me, she shot up into the sky above my head and vanished. I was like she had been sucked upwards. But when I looked up, I couldn't see her or anything else.

Redwood Drive

Date: **10th December 2016**

Time: **02:45am**

Location: **Redwood Drive, Burntwood**

Sighting report:

My house is on Redwood Drive in Burntwood, so that's why I was in my car that evening… or morning, depending on how you look at it.

I'd been visiting family for a few days in Manchester, and I came back home in the early hours to avoid traffic. I was absolutely knackered when I pulled onto the street outside of my house, and I couldn't wait to go inside and get into bed.

I turned the keys to stop my engine, pushed myself back in my seat and stretched for a moment. I took a cigarette out of my pocket and lit it, taking a look around at the street as I did. I noticed something odd.

There was what seemed to look like a little girl just standing between a couple of the cars parked on the street. I looked at her for a moment, and then she must have noticed it because she turned to face me.

I instantly felt a feeling of dread like I do whenever something bad is going to happen. The girl lifted both arms up and pointed her fingers straight at me. When she did that, I felt a feeling go through me like electricity. Honestly, it took my breath away.

I blinked, and the girl was gone. The pain was gone from my body too. I felt my face with my hands to make sure I wasn't dreaming, and relaxed back into my seat feeling confused. It was at that moment that my eyes glanced upwards and met my rear-view mirror. I almost jumped out of my skin as I saw this pale face and black eyes staring right back at me. She was in my car!

I screamed a little and frantically fumbled with the door handle attempting to open it and get out. As I did that, I felt these freezing cold hands touch my shoulder, and I felt even a colder breath near my left ear.

My hands were almost ripping the door off as I tried to get out and save myself. Then the cold air near my ear turned into words.

Now, I don't know what this means, but she whispered into my ear "the end comes after the rain."

And with that, she disappeared entirely and I was able to get out of my car.

This really does feel like some kind of dream now I’m writing it all down, but I know that it wasn't.

Deavall Way

Date: **18th April 2017**

Time: **02:45am**

Location: **Deavall Way, Heath Hayes**

Sighting report:

I'm writing this on behalf of my mom because she's got mobility issues and it's difficult for her to sit at the computer. She is in the room and telling me the story as I write though, and so it should be 100% accurate.

So on 18th April, my mom took a walk to the Chase Garage to get some tobacco at around half two in the morning. She did that often because she doesn't sleep well and she likes an excuse to go outside when everyone else is in bed.

She walked to the garage, which only takes a couple of minutes, bought her tobacco and started heading home. It was then she heard some unearthly noise coming from the small lane at the side of the Newlife shop.

She says she knew it was dangerous following the noise on her own in the dark, but she did it because she was worried someone was in trouble.

She describes the noise as sounding like an evil baby crying (whatever that means?)

My mom walked down the small lane into the darkness following the sound. She says she knew she was getting close to something because the sound was getting louder. Just as she thought she was about to stumble on the cause of the noise, it stopped.

Now my mom was in the middle of a dark lane with no street lights in the pitch black. She started to tremble a little before turning around to make her way back to the main road. When she did that, she saw someone was standing behind her.

This figure was only around 4-feet tall, and so she presumes it must have been a child. She couldn't really see what it looked like because it was so dark, but she says she could feel the cold coming from the person/thing/whatever it was. She said it felt like the figure was sucking all the warmth out of the air.

My mom says she felt panicked and called out "hello?" - the figure didn't respond, but it did jump on the ground. As it jumped, my mom says a shockwave emanated from the place it landed. As if a giant had jumped on the floor, and it almost knocked her over.

The figure then let out the ungodly noise again, this time much louder than before. My mom had to put her hands over her ears and close her eyes, it was so loud. When she opened them again, it was 9:45am, hours had passed, it was light, and she had no idea what happened. Weird ay?

Cardinal Griffin

Date: **21st September 2017**

Time: **03:12am**

Location: **Cardinal Griffin School, Cannock**

Sighting report:

Me and my mates always used to climb over the fence and get onto Cardinal Griffin school field in the early hours. It was a bit of a tradition in fact. We wouldn't cause any damage or do anything wrong. It just felt cool to be somewhere we weren't supposed to be, and it's kinda secluded up there too, so you get left alone.

Anyway, this one night we climbed through the fence (there was a hole on the side near the golf course), sat down on the grass, and started skinning up. We had a little smoke and a couple of beers before my mate Steve said he could see something further into the school field. We were only right at the edge by the fence at this point.

We all turned to see what it was, and to our surprise, there was this girl standing there. Steve said he thought she might be fit but I quickly told him he needed glasses as she was only about ten years old.

All three of us moved towards her to see what she was doing. She wasn't looking in our direction, you see. She was bending down with her back to us as if she was picking or panting something. We were intrigued.

"How's it going?" I shouted over as we got close in an attempt not to startle her. She didn't say anything, but she turned around slowly. You have never seen three lads fall to the ground faster. As she turned around, it was clear to use that she didn't have any eyes!

It was like something out of the Walking Dead and we screamed like little girls ourselves. It looked as though someone had removed her eyes, and all that was left were these black holes.

We started clambering to our feet, and as we did that, the girl lifted off the floor. Like, her feet actually came off the floor. She hovered in the air around a foot from the ground for about ten seconds while we stood there with our mouths open completely stunned.

Steve coughed, and when he did, the girl shot upwards like she was being beamed up to the Starship Enterprise (sorry, Star Trek is my only reference point for something this weird.)

We all looked at each other in disbelief before getting the hell out of there. Steve says he's convinced I spiked his drink or something, but I really didn't.

Gorsemoor Lane

Date: **13th January 2018**

Time: **05:00am**

Location: **Gorsemoor Lane, Heath Hayes**

Sighting report:

I was walking the dog down Goosemoor Lane in Heath Hayes right by the school when I had my encounter with the black eyed child. She appeared from behind the bush at the bottom of the school and seemed to float out into the middle of the path. My dog was terrified, and she's never usually scared of anything.

I'd read in the newspapers about the black eyed child, and so I think I knew that's what I was seeing straight away. The dog shivered behind me, pressed against the back of my leg. The floating girl just stopped in the middle of the path so I would have had no choice but to walk into her if I hadn't have stopped.

Her eyes were pitch black like coal, and she was wearing a sort of little girl's maid outfit.

She wouldn't have looked out of place in a TV program like Downton Abbey or something similar, but her clothes were very dirty.

While there was no light at all coming from her eyes, the girl opened her mouth, and a blinding light shot out that almost made me fall over. It hit me in the face like a brick. I really wasn't expecting it.

The light was so bright that it took around thirty seconds for me to relax my eyes and clear my vision. When I'd done that, the girl was gone, or so I thought.

I suddenly felt someone breathing down my neck. I spun myself around in an instant and saw the girl was now hovering around two feet off the floor directly behind me. When I spun around I was face to face with her.

I saw her mouth opening again, and so I closed my eyes in anticipation of the bright light, but there was no light. Instead, I heard her speak. I couldn't tell what she was saying, but it was something about rain.

When I opened my eyes again, she was gone. I've never seen her since, but I've been telling everyone in the pub this story for months.

Carfax

Date: **22nd October 2018**

Time: **01:50am**

Location: **Carfax, Cannock**

Sighting report:

I have a mate who lives in the flats on the Carfax estate in Cannock. His block is the one with the massive willow tree right outside. It's the only one on the estate, so you won't miss it. I'd often look out of his window at that tree when we were a bit off our heads, and sometimes it used to freak me out.

Anyway, this one night, I'd been at my mate's flat for a few hours and I decided it was time to go home. I said my goodbyes, walked down the stairs, and out of the exit onto the estate. I followed the path until I got to the willow tree and that's when I saw the black eyed girl.

Like I said, that tree always freaked me out, and it had been the cause of more than one panicky feeling over the years.

That was why I paid attention to it, and I always used to take a look as I passed by.

As I got near the tree, I got the usual feeling of sickness in my stomach. However, this time I looked up and saw more than the branches. There she was, the black eyed girl, just sitting in the tree and swinging her feet.

She didn't seem to have any shoes on, just some old, tatty, dress. But I could see her face clearly because of the street lights, and her eyes were definitely black. I've heard people say they feel like she stares into their soul, and that's what it felt like for me too. It was like the whole world stopped. Everything went silent. There was just me and her.

In a flash, she jumped down out of the tree and landed on the ground in front of me with a thud. It was strange. The ground shook as if she weighed half a ton, not about five stone. I started shaking more.

I don't know why I did this, but I looked down at my watch and noticed it had stopped working. The time was fixed at 01.50am. The girl then turned away from me and began to walk (I saw walk, but it seemed more like gliding) away from me. About ten metres away, she turned and did a "come this way" motion with her finger. I was definitely NOT going that way.

I'm a bit ashamed to say it after seeing something so incredible with my own eyes, but I ran as fast as I could in the opposite direction and never looked back.

Kingies Rock

Date: **4th January 2019**

Time: **02:10am**

Location: **Kingies Rock, Hednesford**

Sighting report:

You know where Kingies Rock is, right? It's on the Littleworth Road between Kingsmead School and the Trafalgar pub. You can't miss it. It's like this thirty-foot standing red rock at the side of the road. School kids often climb it. I did when I was at school anyway.

It's a cool place to get some good views of Heath Hayes all the way to Five Ways island, and people sit up there to eat a picnic sometimes.

Well, I was walking past there this one night when I think I saw a black eyed kid or child or whatever they are. It looked like it was standing on the rock looking at the view like everyone else does, but when I got a bit closer, I noticed it's feet weren't on the ground.

In fact, it's body wasn't even above the rock, it was out to the side of it just floating in thin air. I couldn't believe my eyes. I'd have said it looked like some sort of angel if I didn't know better.

You know when Reagan from the Exorcist floats up from the bed? Yeah, well this thing looked like that except it was floating vertically instead of horizontally. I tried to get in closer to take some photos with my phone, but as soon as the flash went off the black eyed girl started to make this squealing noise, now starting right at me.

I stumbled over some overgrowth as I tried to get out of the way and back to the road but it was no use. The creature flew down like something out of a horror movie and positioned itself between me and the road. I could hear it breathing, but it sounded heavy like when you have a cold.

I asked the ghost or whatever it was what it wanted, but that just seemed to make it angrier. I thought I heard it speak for a moment, but thinking back, that might have been the wind. Who knows?

Before I could do or say anything else, the creature started floating towards me fast. I put my hands up to protect myself because it was coming towards me at some considerable speed. Just as I thought it was going to smash into me, I closed my eyes.

A few seconds passed before I opened them, but when I did, it was light outside and the black eyed girl was gone. I checked my watch and saw it was 8:45am.

I could see school kids rushing and trying not to be late for registration. I'd been out there for hours, and I have no memory of what happened after the girl was moving towards me.

I didn't feel her hit me. Maybe she flew over me? Perhaps she flew through me or took me somewhere? I have no idea. I just know I'm still confused and I lost around 6 hours that morning.

Rugeley Road

Date: **16th May 2019**

Time: **03:30am**

Location: **Rugeley Road, Hednesford**

Sighting report:

I was driving down the Rugeley Road, and I picked up a weird hitchhiker who I think might have been that black-eyed thing everyone is talking about in the newspapers.

She was just standing at the side of the road in the darkness, and so I decided to stop and offer her a lift. The strange thing was, I don't think she actually opened my back door to get into the car. I didn't hear it open anyway.

I pulled up alongside her, asked if she needed a lift, and the next thing I know, she's in the back seat. I have no memory of her climbing in, and I remember it making me feel uneasy at the time too.

I tried to make small talk but she didn't reply to anything I said as we drove along the road. I decided to take a look in the rear view mirror, and what I saw made me go white. I had a girl in the back of my car with wet black hair, pale skin, and no eyes. Literally no eyes! It was like they'd been surgically removed.

I slammed my foot down on my break when I saw those holes in her head, and it caused my car to swerve off the road and into a ditch. I think I was knocked out for a couple of minutes before I came round and managed to climb out of the passenger door. The girl was nowhere to be seen. I think she might have made me crash on purpose.

I called the Police and a recovery company, but I couldn't tell the truth to either of them. I was shook up enough without being handcuffed and forced to undergo a mental health assessment, so I kept my mouth shut. I told the Police I saw a badger in the middle of the road, and that's why I swerved and crashed. I just didn't want to face the ridicule of being known as the bloke who thinks a ghost made him crash his car.

I don't travel down that road at night any more. It's just too spooky out there.

Pye Green Tower

Date: **26th October 2019**

Time: **04:30am**

Location: **Pye Green Tower, Hednesford**

Sighting report:

I like to walk around the old German War cemetery sometimes when I'm out with my dog, and that's what I was doing a few days before Halloween in 2019. I'd already been around the cemetery, and I was walking with the dog back to our house in Pye Green.

As we got close to the famous Pye Green tower, my dog started pulling at its lead like crazy. I thought it was going to snap if I told you the truth. The dog was trying to pull me into the trees right by the tower. I asked what he could see or smell, but he's a dog, so obviously, he didn't tell me.

Still, I went along with it to see what we were going to find. Just then, a specter appeared out of the tree line. My dog didn't seem so brave any more, and he started to yelp a little bit.

The apparition was about ten feet in front of us, and only around four feet from the floor. That made me instantly realise it was a child, or at least something of child size and shape. The dog remained scared.

Before I could say or do anything, the figure begane to slide across the floor and move towards us. It was like she had ice skates or something like that. Really smooth movement and no footstep sounds.

As she moved closer, I could see this was a girl, only she looked like she'd been beaten up. Her eyes looked entirely black. I didn't have my glasses on, so I couldn't see properly, but she either had huge black eyes, or she had the other kind of black eyes from fighting or something. Either way, I couldn't see any white in her eyes and I felt uneasy.

The girl lifted even higher off the floor as she got really closer to me until she was face to face with me. Her feet must have been around three-feet off the ground at least for her face to be the same height as mine. I'm almost 7-feet tall myself.

I could see her face a lot more by this point, and I know this makes me sound mental, but it was like I could see through her skin. It was then she said something and I heard her voice. I'll never forget this because it sounded like some mad quote you'd hear in a horror film, but in a really quiet voice, the girl said "the rain is coming." And with that, the heavens opened instantly, and me and my dog got soaked.

The black eyed girl was gone, and the downpour lasted for a good ten minutes before clearing up. I just wish this had happened during the day so I'd have got a better idea of what she looked like. I'm an artist you see. I could draw her if I'd been able to see her better.

Stafford Road

Date: **14th February 2020**

Time: **02:00am**

Location: **Stafford Road, Cannock**

Sighting report:

I have retold my account to my friends and family but it falls on deaf ears as none of them believe me and they accuse me of lying. I almost wish that I was lying as the events that happened to me are unexplainable and still terrify me in my dreams. A friend recommended I get in touch with you as you are the expert on the Black Eyed Child of Cannock Chase and I really hope that you help me understand and make sense of my experience.

It was a cold and snowy day in early spring this year, I remember it clearly as I had a lot to do that day and I wasn't happy that it was snowing as this would just slow me down. A few hours into my day, I was driving down Stafford Road through the forest in Cannock Chase. The snow was blinding on the road so I was taking it very cautiously and I noticed the snow had just begun to melt causing the roads to become more slippery.

I was busy concentrating on the road when my eyes were drawn to a figure moving in the woods. I first presumed it was just a child making the most of the weather and playing in the snow. However when I looked again, I could see the figure more clearly and it appeared to be a small childlike figure, wearing an old fashioned black dress. I guess that's the reason I noticed her in the first place as the black dress stood out in sharp contrast to the snow.

The roads were dangerous that day so I could only glance into the woods for a few seconds at a time, I could have easily slid the car and lost control if I wasn't careful. As I got closer I could see that the girl wasn’t playing in the snow, she appeared to be alone and was standing very still with her eyes locked on my car.

My gut reaction was then to think perhaps she was lost or in distress and I immediately slowed down and signalled to pull over. I stopped just ahead of where the girl was so I could see her in my mirrors as I parked up. I quickly turned my engine off and got out of the car, but when I turned around to see the girl she was gone.

Thinking perhaps she had run away I walked up and down the road for a few minutes to see if I could spot her in the woods. I considered that she may have hidden away somewhere so I shouted “hey - are you okay? Are you lost? It's not safe to be in these woods on your own”, but no one replied.

Feeling a bit confused and deflated I got back into my car. I started to question myself and I wondered if I had seen anyone there at all.

I tried to convince myself that it was a trick of the light after being blinded by the snow, and it was probably just a hedge or a shadow. I started my engine and slowly pulled the car away. I kept a close eye on the woods as I drove along slowly, hoping to see a similar trick of the light or figure shaped hedge or the girl again to reassure me that I'm not going crazy.

I was tentatively trying to watch the road and scan the woods at the same time as I was slowly travelling down the road.

My concentration was suddenly broken by the sound of a quiet and childlike giggle coming from my back seat. The noise terrified me and I jumped so violently I swerved the car and struggled to keep it on the road. My eyes flew to the interior mirror and I saw the same little girl in the black dress from the woods earlier sat in the back of my car. Her face was white as a ghost and eyes were black as coal. It was her eyes that scared me the most as they didn't seem natural. I couldn't see any white in her eyes yet I knew she was staring right at me, almost feeling like she was staring through me.

Thankfully it only took me a few seconds to regain control of the car and slam the brakes, all the while I could see the black eyed girl in the interior mirror. As soon as I had stopped the car, I unbuckled my seatbelt as I turned around to face the girl in the back seat. However when I had turned she was gone. The doors were still closed so she did not exit the car and I leant over to see if she was behind my seat but she was not there.

I got out of the car and opened the back seat doors to check again. She was definitely not in the vehicle. I walked around the whole car checking it frantically.

I also scanned the woods around me in case she had somehow got out without me seeing, but she wasn't there either. I really thought I was going mad at this point. I knew that I had definitely seen something this time and it wasn't an illusion or trick of the light because I had seen her eyes so clearly and I heard her giggle.

After a few minutes I managed to calm myself down enough to get back in the car and drive home. I was almost too scared to do that but the thought of staying in the woods was much scarier. I told a few of my family and friends about it afterwards but like I said none of them believe me.

Afterword

I hope you found this small selection of sighting reports interesting, and that you now understand quite how common sightings of the black eyed child are in Cannock Chase.

You have just read only a fraction of the sighting reports I have in my files. If you have any opinions on the black eyed child and what you think it might be, please feel free to get in touch. You can find my contact details online.

Also, if you haven't done so already, you can get my original book UFOs, Werewolves, & the Pig-Man from Amazon and other places online. That book delves more deeply into other paranormal and UFO sightings in the Cannock Chase area.

I hope to hear from you soon!

Lee

Printed in Great Britain
by Amazon

11359724R00031